BIOGRAPHIES OF DIVERSE HEROES
KAMALA HARRIS

STEPHANIE GASTON

TABLE OF CONTENTS

Kamala Harris...3

Glossary... 22

Index.. 22

A Crabtree Seedlings Book

School-to-Home Support for Caregivers and Teachers

This book helps children grow by letting them practice reading. Here are a few guiding questions to help the reader with building his or her comprehension skills. Possible answers appear here in red.

Before Reading:

- What do I think this book is about?
  - *I think this book is about Kamala Harris being the first woman vice president of the United States.*
  - *I think this book will be about the experiences that influenced Kamala Harris.*

- What do I want to learn about this topic?
  - *I want to learn about where Kamala Harris grew up and her family life.*
  - *I want to learn about why Kamala Harris pursued a career in the law and politics.*

During Reading:

- I wonder why…
  - *I wonder why Kamala Harris is called a first-generation American.*
  - *I wonder why Kamala Harris wanted to run for the elected position of attorney general of California.*

- What have I learned so far?
  - *I have learned that Kamala Harris launched a presidential bid in January of 2019 but dropped out of the race.*
  - *I have learned that former Vice President Joe Biden picked Kamala Harris to be his running mate.*

After Reading:

- What details did I learn about this topic?
  - *I have learned that Kamala Harris officially became the vice president of the United States on January 20, 2021.*
  - *I have learned that Kamala Harris's first name honors her Indian background.*

- Read the book again and look for the glossary words.
  - *I see the word **motivated** on page 8 and the word **nomination** on page 14. The other glossary words are found on page 22.*

KAMALA HARRIS

Kamala Harris is the first woman, first Black person, and first South Asian to become vice president of the United States.

Harris was born in Oakland, California, on October 20, 1964.

Harris and her younger sister are **first-generation** Americans.

Harris's childhood home

Harris's mother was from India, and her father is from Jamaica.

 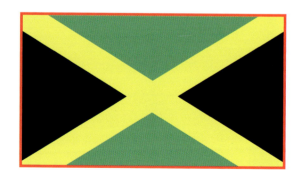

Kamala's first name honors her Indian background.

Harris would attend **civil rights** protests with her parents as a young girl.

Those protests **motivated** her to choose a career in law.

Harris delivered remarks on the 50th anniversary of the signing of the Civil Rights Act.

Harris graduated from Howard University with a degree in political science.

She later attended law school at the University of California at Hastings.

In 2003, Harris was elected district attorney of San Francisco.

And in 2010, she was elected attorney general of California.

Harris launched her presidential **campaign** in January of 2019.

Her aim was to win the **nomination** for the Democratic presidential candidate.

Nearly one year later, Harris ended her campaign. She explained that it did not have enough money to continue.

However, some predicted that Harris would still be on the ballot.

Federal Offices

President and Vice President
Vote for One

○ **Republican**
Donald J Trump
Michael R Pence

○ **Democrat**
Joseph R Biden
Kamala D Harris

○ **Libertarian**
Jo Jorgensen
Jeremy (Spike) Cohen

○ **Pacific Green**
Howie Hawkins
Angela Walker

○ **Progressive**
Dario Hunter
Neptune Adams

Former Vice President Joe Biden later won the nomination for the Democratic presidential candidate.

He chose Harris to be his running mate.

Joe Biden served as vice president of the United States from 2009–2017.

Biden and Harris won the presidential election in November of 2020.

Harris officially became the vice president of the United States on January 20, 2021.

Glossary

campaign (kam-peyn): The competition between rival political candidates for public office

civil rights (siv-uhl rahyts): The rights of citizens to political and social freedom and equality

first-generation (furst-jen-uh-rey-shuhn): The first generation of a family to be born in a particular country

motivated (moh-tuh-veyt-id): To have a reason for doing something

nomination (nom-uh-ney-shuhn): The official naming of someone to be in the running for an election

Index

Biden, Joe 18, 20
California 4, 11, 12
campaign 14, 16, 18, 20
civil rights 8, 9

Howard University 10
India 6, 7
Jamaica 6

❝The American dream belongs to all of us.❞

—Kamala Harris

About the Author

Stephanie Gaston is a content producer for CNN and a screenwriter. She spent more than a decade working for the FOX and ABC affiliates in Miami, Florida, before joining the ranks at CNN in 2015, ahead of an unprecedented election cycle. Stephanie is a first-generation Haitian American who grew up in Fort Lauderdale, Florida, a diverse community with Latin and Caribbean influences. Throughout her career in journalism, Stephanie has covered major stories including presidential inaugurations, natural disasters, and royal weddings. Stephanie is a dog lover, movie buff, fitness enthusiast, and most importantly, a proud mom.

Written by: Stephanie Gaston
Designed by: Under the Oaks Media
Proofreader: Petrice Custance
Print coordinator: Katherine Berti

Photographs: Lawrence Jackson: cover, p. 3; Cullen 328: p. 5; MazDay: p. 6 (left); petch one: p. 6 (right); LOC: p. 8; Seth Taylor: p. 9; Archivo GBB: p. 10; Chinnapong: p. 11; Office of the Attorney General of California; Sgeila Fitzgerald: p. 15; Echo Visuals: p. 17; Sam Shore: p. 19; Adam Schultz: p. 21

Library and Archives Canada Cataloguing in Publication

Available at the Library and Archives Canada

Library of Congress Cataloging-in-Publication Data

Available at the Library of Congress

Crabtree Publishing Company

www.crabtreebooks.com   1-800-387-7650

Copyright © 2023 **CRABTREE PUBLISHING COMPANY**

All rights reserved. No part of this publication may be reproduced, stored in a retrieval system or be transmitted in any form or by any means, electronic, mechanical, photocopying, recording, or otherwise, without the prior written permission of Crabtree Publishing Company. In Canada: We acknowledge the financial support of the Government of Canada through the Canada Book Fund for our publishing activities.

Published in the United States
Crabtree Publishing
347 Fifth Avenue
Suite 1402-145
New York, NY, 10016

Published in Canada
Crabtree Publishing
616 Welland Ave.
St. Catharines, ON
L2M 5V6

Printed in the U.S.A./072022/CG20220201